salads

salads

Elsa Petersen-Schepelern

photography by Peter Cassidy

RYLAND
PETERS
& SMALL

LONDON NEW YORK

Designer Vicky Holmes

Editors Maddalena Bastianelli, Erica Marcus

Production Patricia Harrington

Art Director Gabriella Le Grazie

Publishing Director Alison Starling

Food Stylist Louise Pickford

Stylist Wei Tang

Photographer's Assistant Rachel Tomlinson

First published in the United States in 2001
by Ryland Peters & Small, Inc.,
519 Broadway, 5th Floor
New York, NY 10012
10 9 8
www.rylandpeters.com

Text © Elsa Petersen-Schepelern 2001
Design and photographs © Ryland Peters & Small 2001

Printed and bound in China

ISBN 1 84172 164 6

Author's acknowledgments

My thanks to my sister Kirsten, my nephews Peter Bray and Luc Votan (for his expert advice on
Vietnamese food), my cousins in Italy—Nowelle and Clemente Valentino-Capezza and their daughters
Veronica and Tina. Thanks also to Sheridan Lear the "Preserving Princess," to Erica Marcus for her
wise advice, and Susan Stuck, Maggie Ramsay and Maddie Bastianelli, as ever. Halcyon Herbs
provided the incredible salad leaves and herbs—to them, my heartfelt thanks. Thanks also to the
brilliant Louise Pickford for her light touch with food styling, to Vicky Walters, to photographer
Peter Cassidy who just takes my breath away, to Wei Tang and her deft eye for styling, and
to Vicky Holmes for her beautiful design.

Notes

All spoon measurements are level unless otherwise noted. Ovens should be preheated to the
specified temperature. Recipes in this book were tested with a convection oven. If using a
regular oven, increase the cooking times according to the manufacturer's instructions.

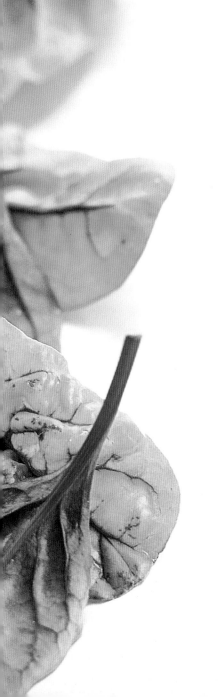

contents

there's more to salads than just green...

Salads mean summer—and winter too. In this book, I have given a choice of salads for all seasons and occasions: for a light snack or a substantial meal, to serve as an appetizer, or as a palate-cleanser between the entrée and the cheese. There's even a fruit salad to serve at the end of a meal.

A salad is the sort of thing I like to take to work: homemade is always nicer, cheaper, and fresher than the sort you buy from salad bars.

The dressing makes a huge difference to a salad. I'm a great fan of simple vinaigrettes—preferably mostly oil and very little vinegar. Experiment with oils: try assertively flavored extra virgin olive oils from different regions—or nut oils such as walnut, hazelnut, or macadamia (you may need to mellow their flavors with a mild olive oil) and then there are the seed oils, such as pumpkin or sesame, which can be very strong indeed and should be used like a

seasoning rather than a dressing. The same might be said for balsamic vinegar—use just a few drops, not a heavy hand.

The choice of vinegars or citrus juices depends very much on personal taste. I usually choose either mild white rice vinegar or the complex flavors of vinegars made from sherry or cider. Lemon is the smoothest of the citrus juices, lime more fragrant, and orange of course sweeter. Whatever the acidic component, I prefer it to be minimal, in a ratio of 5 or 6 parts oil to 1 of vinegar. If you need to put sugar in a vinaigrette, you've probably used too much vinegar.

Try spicy dressings from Southeast Asia, your favorite Green Goddess, flavor-packed pesto, or unctuous mayonnaise. It's really no trouble to make your own mayonnaise, and the ingredients are very simple—unlike store-bought versions, which always taste too vinegary, too sweet, too chemical. Give me homemade every time.

...though green is a good place to start! Salads can be cold or cool, warm or hot, but they should always include a delicious combination of various flavors, textures, and colors.

LEAVES AND HERBS

Caesar salad

Classic Caesar Salad includes either a raw or 1-minute egg, but this is out of bounds for many people these days. Instead, I make it with a soft-boiled 4-minute egg. My idea of 4 minutes is timed from when the water starts to boil. If you would prefer a hard-cooked egg, by all means simmer it a little longer—just 2 minutes more will make it hard-cooked.

6–8 smallest leaves of a young romaine lettuce

2 tablespoons extra virgin olive oil

½ tablespoon freshly squeezed lemon juice, plus 1 lemon, cut into wedges

kosher salt or sea salt flakes and freshly ground black pepper

CROUTONS

1 thick slice brioche, challah bread, or white bread

about 2 tablespoons oil and/or butter, for cooking

1 large garlic clove, smashed

TO SERVE

3–4 anchovy fillets, preferably salt-packed, rinsed

1 soft-cooked (1-minute or 4-minute) egg, peeled, and halved or quartered

Parmesan cheese, shaved into curls with a vegetable peeler

SERVES 1

To make the croutons, toast the slice of bread or brioche lightly on both sides. Cut into big cubes, cutting off and discarding the crusts first.

Heat the oil and/or butter in a skillet and add the garlic. Add the cubes of bread and cook, turning frequently, until golden on all sides. Discard the garlic after about 1 minute—do not let it burn. When the cubes are golden, remove and drain on paper towels.

Put the lettuce leaves in a large bowl and sprinkle with the olive oil. Using your hands, roll the leaves in the oil. Sprinkle with lemon juice and roll again.

Put the croutons into a bowl and put the dressed leaves on top. Sprinkle with salt and lots of freshly ground black pepper. Add the anchovies, egg, and shavings of Parmesan and serve.

Note: If you don't like anchovies, omit them, and add 1 teaspoon Worcestershire sauce or a pinch of salt with the olive oil.

Green salad

Any book on salads must include a classic green salad. I think you must stick with green—have no truck with tomatoes and bell peppers and things of that nature. Choose a combination of leaves—some crisp, some bitter, some peppery, some soft. The perfection of the dressing is what's important. My view is that the oil must be as marvelous as possible and the vinegar as little as possible. I also prefer it without mustard or garlic, but please yourself.

smallest leaves from 1 romaine lettuce heart, torn

leaves from 1 Belgian endive

1 bunch arugula

2 cups mesclun leaves

1 bunch watercress, trimmed, about 3 oz.

your choice of other leaves, such as young dandelion leaves, young nasturtium leaves, young flat-leaf parsley

DRESSING

½ garlic clove (optional)

a pinch of kosher salt or sea salt flakes

6 parts extra virgin olive oil

1 part vinegar, such as white rice, sherry, white or red wine, or cider

1 teaspoon Dijon mustard (optional)

freshly ground black pepper

SERVES 4–6

Wash the leaves as necessary and spin dry in a salad spinner. Put in plastic bags and chill for at least 30 minutes to make the leaves crisp. (If washing soft leaves like mesclun, do it at the last minute, otherwise they will go mushy.)

If using garlic, put it on a board with a pinch of salt and crush thoroughly with the back of a heavy knife (use a garlic crusher if you must, but I think the texture is better this way.) Transfer to a salad bowl, add the olive oil, vinegar, mustard, if using, and pepper, then beat with a fork or small whisk.

When ready to serve, add the leaves and, using your hands, turn them gently in the dressing until lightly coated. (I prefer to use my hands—they don't bruise the leaves and you can make sure everything is well coated.)

Note: A few tablespoons of dressing is plenty for a salad of this size—too much will spoil it. I prefer the vinegar to be as gentle as possible. (White rice vinegar is my current favorite.)

Tatsoi, avocado, and frisée
with croutons and pancetta

2 cups tatsoi or mesclun, loosely packed

1 frisée, leaves separated

6 thinly cut slices pancetta or bacon

1 ripe Hass avocado

½ tablespoon olive oil, for cooking

CROUTONS

2 garlic cloves, crushed

6 thick slices white bread

clarified butter or olive oil, for cooking

DRESSING

6 tablespoons extra virgin olive oil

1 tablespoon sherry vinegar or rice vinegar

½ garlic clove, crushed

a few drops of balsamic vinegar

salt and freshly ground black pepper

SERVES 4

Tatsoi is a crisp baby Chinese leaf sold in many markets. It's like a mini bok choy leaf. It's good in stir-fries, but even better as a salad leaf. If you can't find it, use watercress. Balsamic vinegar is a terrific ingredient, but I think most people use too much of it. Use just a few drops to contrast with the creaminess of avocado, which in turn should be scooped out with a teaspoon—when sliced, it loses much of its appeal. This salad is delicious as an appetizer.

Wash the tatsoi and frisée leaves and dry in a salad spinner. Put in a plastic bag and chill.

To make the croutons, rub the garlic over the bread. Remove the crusts and cut the bread into cubes. Heat the clarified butter or olive oil in a skillet or deep fryer, add the cubes of bread, and sauté or deep-fry or sauté until light brown. Drain on paper towels.

Heat a skillet, brush with the ½ tablespoon olive oil, add the pancetta or bacon, and cook at a medium-high heat, without disturbing the slices, until crisp on one side. Using tongs, turn the slices over and sauté until the other side is crisp. Remove and drain on paper towels, then cut into 2-inch lengths.

Put the dressing ingredients in a salad bowl and beat with a fork or small whisk. When ready to serve, add the leaves and turn in the dressing, using your hands. Cut the avocado in half and remove the stone. Using a teaspoon, scoop out balls of avocado into the salad. Add the crisp pancetta or bacon and serve.

Blue cheese salad
with crisp bacon and pine nuts

2 tablespoons pine nuts

1 tablespoon olive oil, for cooking

12 thinly cut slices bacon or pancetta

4 oz. dolcelatte, Roquefort, or other blue cheese, diced, about ½ cup

3 tablespoons extra virgin olive oil, or to taste

1 tablespoon white rice vinegar or freshly squeezed lemon juice, or to taste

mixed salad leaves, including peppery leaves like watercress, arugula, and mustard, bitter ones like frisée, soft ones like Bibb or Boston lettuce, and herb sprigs

1 Hass avocado, scooped into balls with a teaspoon (optional)

kosher salt or sea salt flakes and freshly ground black pepper

SERVES 4

This salad of herbs and mixed leaves—peppery, soft, and bitter—is dressed with a creamy blue cheese dressing. I often serve it at weekday dinner parties because it covers three courses in one; appetizer, salad, and cheese.

Put the pine nuts in a dry skillet and sauté for about 1–2 minutes only, until golden—shake and stir several times to prevent them from burning. Set aside.

Heat the olive oil in the skillet, add the bacon or pancetta, and sauté until crisp. Drain on a plate lined with paper towels.

Put the cheese in a large salad bowl and crumble well with a fork. Add the extra virgin olive oil and vinegar or lemon juice. Mash, then beat to a loose and creamy consistency, adding water if necessary—alternatively, use a hand-held stick blender. Add salt and lots of freshly ground black pepper to taste.

Put the salad leaves on top of the cheese dressing, then add the avocado, if using. Sprinkle with the bacon or pancetta and pine nuts (scrape any crunchy bits from the pan into the bowl too.)

Serve in the salad bowl for guests to help themselves, or make in 4 separate bowls, dividing the ingredients as appropriate. Lots of wine and crusty bread are perfect accompaniments.

This version of the famous salad was taught to me by a Lebanese doctor, who is most particular about his tabbouleh. The most important thing to remember is that this is a parsley and mint salad, not a bulgur wheat or even a couscous salad as is so often seen. There should be so much green that you hardly notice the grain—or the tomatoes.

Lebanese tabbouleh

Soak the bulgur wheat in water for 20 minutes, then drain. Peel, seed, and chop the tomatoes, then chop the parsley and mint.

Put the tomatoes, herbs, scallions, and bulgur wheat in a bowl. Sprinkle with the olive oil and lemon juice and toss well. Season to taste.

Serve with lemon halves, pita bread, and other Lebanese appetizers or mezze dishes.

⅔ cup medium bulgur wheat

2 large ripe red tomatoes

a bunch of flat-leaf parsley

a large bunch of mint

3 scallions, sliced

2 tablespoons fruity extra virgin olive oil

1 tablespoon freshly squeezed lemon juice

kosher salt or sea salt and freshly cracked black pepper

SERVES 4

VEGETABLES

Pumpkin oil is a favorite of mine, dark green, toasty, and nutty—and you need far less than any other oil. It's supposed to be good for you, but frankly it tastes so good that I wouldn't mind if it were as sinful as chocolate. If you can't find it, omit from this salad and make the dressing without it. Microwaving green vegetables keeps them crisp and green, but you can also steam or blanch them.

Green vegetable salad
with pumpkin oil dressing

about 12 baby asparagus tips

a handful of French green beans (haricots verts), untrimmed

4 baby zucchini, cut in thirds lengthwise (optional)

1½ cups sugar snap peas

1 cup frozen green peas, thawed

6–8 scallions, as small as possible

kosher salt or sea salt flakes and freshly cracked black pepper

fresh Parmesan cheese, to serve

PUMPKIN OIL DRESSING

6 parts extra virgin olive oil

1 part Japanese rice vinegar or white wine vinegar

½ teaspoon Dijon mustard

a little kosher salt or sea salt and freshly cracked black pepper

pumpkin oil, to taste (optional)

SERVES 4

Microwave the asparagus tips, beans, zucchini, sugar snaps, and green peas separately on high for 2 minutes each, then transfer immediately to a bowl of ice cubes and water. This stops them cooking and sets the color.

To make the dressing, put the olive oil, vinegar, mustard, salt, and pepper in a screw-top bottle and shake well to form an emulsion. Put in a bowl, add the drained vegetables, one kind at a time, and toss until lightly coated. Arrange the asparagus, zucchini, and scallions on a serving platter or 4 rectangular salad plates. Add the sugar snaps and green peas, then sprinkle with pumpkin oil (you don't need much—its flavor is very assertive). Shave fresh Parmesan over the top and sprinkle with salt and cracked black pepper.

Alter the vegetable components of this salad according to what's in season. Try broccoli or carrots sliced lengthwise into matchsticks, spinach leaves, sliced Chinese cabbage, or cauliflower florets. I like Chinese long beans rather than ordinary beans for salads, because they keep their crunch better.

Indonesian gado-gado

2 small cucumbers, such as Kirby, halved lengthwise and seeded

8 Chinese long beans or green beans, cut into 2-inch lengths

1 orange or red bell pepper

2 firm tofu cakes

20–25 shrimp crackers (optional)

2 red onions, finely sliced into rings

a large handful of bean sprouts, rinsed, drained, and trimmed

8 small leaves romaine lettuce

6 inches daikon, peeled and sliced into matchstick lengths

2 hard-cooked eggs, quartered

kosher salt or sea salt flakes

peanut oil, for cooking

PEANUT SAUCE

1½ cups shelled fresh peanuts

2 red chiles, halved, seeded, and finely chopped

2 bird eye chiles, halved, seeded, and finely chopped

1 onion, finely chopped

1 garlic clove, crushed

1 teaspoon kosher salt or sea salt

2 teaspoons brown sugar

⅔ cup coconut milk

SERVES 4

To make the peanut sauce, toast the peanuts in a dry skillet. Transfer to a dish towel, rub off the skins, then put the nuts in a blender. Grind to a coarse meal, then add the chiles, onion, garlic, salt, sugar, and coconut milk. Blend to a purée, then transfer to a saucepan and cook, stirring, until thickened.

Finely slice the halved cucumbers diagonally, put on a plate, sprinkle with salt, set aside for 10 minutes, then rinse and pat dry with paper towels. Chill.

Cook the beans in boiling salted water until *al dente*, then drain, rinse immediately under cold running water, then transfer to a bowl of ice water. Just before serving, drain again and pat dry with paper towels.

Peel the pepper with a vegetable peeler, cut off and discard the top and bottom, then halve, seed, and finely slice lengthwise.

Heat 2 tablespoons of the peanut oil in a skillet, add the tofu, and cook until brown on both sides, then drain and slice thickly.

To cook the shrimp crackers, fill a wok or heavy kettle one-third full with peanut oil and heat to 375°F. Drop in 1 cracker to test the temperature—it should puff up immediately. Add the crackers, crowding them so they curl up, then cook until puffed and golden, about 3 seconds. Remove and drain on paper towels.

To cook the onion rings, reheat the oil, add the sliced onion and deep-fry until crisp and golden. Remove and drain on paper towels.

Arrange the cucumbers, beans, pepper, tofu, bean sprouts, lettuce leaves, daikon, and quartered eggs on a large platter. Top with the onion rings and shrimp crackers, drizzle with the peanut sauce, sprinkle with salt, and serve.

Warm roasted vegetable salad
with goat cheese and pesto

Gorgeous with your choice of roasted vegetables. My favorite is pumpkin—and I also include tomatoes to act as a sauce.

2 red and 2 yellow bell peppers, halved and seeded

1 lb. green-skinned pumpkin (winter squash), peeled, but with seeds intact, cut into 1-inch wedges

2 sweet potatoes, cut into 1-inch chunks

2 red onions, quartered lengthwise into wedges

½ cup extra virgin olive oil, plus extra for brushing and drizzling

a handful of basil leaves

4 cherry tomatoes, halved

8 teaspoons pesto (page 61)

about 4 oz. mature goat cheese, cut into 8 chunks

4 medium tomatoes, halved

kosher salt or sea salt flakes and freshly ground black pepper

lemon wedges, to serve

SERVES 4–6

Put all the vegetables except the tomatoes in a plastic bag, add the olive oil, salt, and pepper, then shake until everything is well coated in oil.

Brush a large roasting pan with more oil and add the peppers, cut side up. Put a basil leaf, a halved cherry tomato, a spoonful of pesto, and a chunk of goat cheese in each pepper half. Drizzle more olive oil over the top.

Add the pumpkin, sweet potatoes, red onions, and medium tomatoes, leaving space around each piece.

Preheat the oven to 450°F. Add the pan and roast the vegetables for 30 minutes or until tender right through and crispy brown at the edges.

Serve with extra fresh basil leaves and wedges of lemon. Toasted or grilled ciabatta or focaccia is also delicious. A hands-on dish.

Three potato salad
with chives and parsley

1 lb. small blue potatoes

1 lb. red new potatoes

1 lb. baby yellow or white potatoes

1 tablespoon olive oil

a bunch of flat-leaf parsley, leaves finely chopped

a bunch of chives, snipped with kitchen shears

VINAIGRETTE

5 tablespoons extra virgin olive oil (the best you can find)

1 tablespoon sherry vinegar

1 teaspoon Dijon mustard

kosher salt or sea salt and freshly ground black pepper

SERVES 4

Put all the vinaigrette ingredients in a screw-top bottle and shake until emulsified—put more salt in the dressing than usual, since you will have steamed the potatoes rather than boiling them in salted water.

Steam all the potatoes until tender, with the skins just beginning to split. (I steam them in separate layers of a bamboo steamer, since they are inclined to cook at different rates.) Dunk immediately into ice water to cool. Cut the blue potatoes in half and slip off the skins (this will show off the color better.)

Drain the red and yellow or white potatoes and pat dry with paper towels. Put 1 tablespoon of olive oil in a bowl, add all the potatoes and toss gently to coat. Transfer to a salad bowl, drizzle with the vinaigrette, and sprinkle with parsley and chives.

I love this salad because I absolutely adore the smoky, earthy taste of blue potatoes. They have a very short season and can be hard to find, but, if you do, make a fuss of them like this. If unavailable, use extra potatoes of either of the other colors.

Tuscan panzanella

There are as many variations of this Tuscan bread salad as there are cooks. The secret is to let the flavors blend well without letting the bread disintegrate into a mush. Make this when local tomatoes are in season, and always use the ripest, reddest, most flavorful ones you can find—sweet "marmande," with its furrowed skin is my favorite.

6 very ripe plum tomatoes

2 garlic cloves, sliced into slivers

4 thick slices chewy day-old bread, preferably Italian-style such as pugliese or ciabatta

about 4 inches cucumber, halved, seeded, and finely sliced diagonally

1 red onion, diced

1 tablespoon chopped fresh flat-leaf parsley

½–¾ cup extra virgin olive oil

2 tablespoons white wine vinegar, cider vinegar, or sherry vinegar

1 teaspoon balsamic vinegar (optional)

a bunch of basil, leaves torn

12 caperberries or ¼ cup capers packed in brine, rinsed and drained

kosher salt or sea salt and freshly ground black pepper

SERVES 4

Preheat the oven to 350°F. Cut the tomatoes in half, insert slivers of garlic, and roast in the oven for about 1 hour, or until wilted and some of the moisture has evaporated.

Meanwhile, put the bread on an oiled stove-top grill pan and cook until lightly toasted and barred with grill marks on both sides. Alternatively, toast lightly under a broiler. Tear or cut the toast into pieces and put into a salad bowl. Sprinkle with a little water until damp.

Add the tomatoes, cucumber, onion, parsley, salt, and pepper. Sprinkle with the olive oil and vinegar, toss well, then set aside for about 1 hour to develop the flavors.

Add the basil leaves and caperberries or capers and serve.

FISH CHICKEN AND MEAT

Smoked salmon salad

The salty, smoky taste of salmon blends well with the starchy texture of potatoes. Fava beans, also known as broad beans, are one of the few foods that don't seem to suffer from the freezing process. In fact, since they're frozen almost as soon as they're picked, their texture can often be better than those you buy fresh—these might have been harvested days earlier and their natural sweetness turns to starch very quickly after picking. Like most green vegetables, fava beans are very good cooked in a microwave.

2 cups shelled fava beans, shelled (about 7 lb. unshelled) or green peas, fresh or frozen

12 red new potatoes

4–5 tablespoons extra virgin olive oil

4 oz. smoked salmon, diced`

a handful of fresh chives, snipped or chopped

4 teaspoons cider vinegar, white wine vinegar or rice vinegar

kosher salt or sea salt and cracked black pepper

SERVES 4

Microwave the fava beans on full for 3 minutes if fresh or 2 minutes if frozen. If using peas, microwave for about 1 minute only. Transfer immediately to a bowl of ice water. When cold, pop them out of their gray skins, discard the skins, and reserve the beans. (You can also cook the beans or peas in boiling water instead of a microwave.)

Boil the potatoes whole in their skins until tender, about 15-20 minutes (the time depends on the size of the potatoes.) Drain, then toss in 2-3 teaspoons of the olive oil (gently so as not to break the skins.) Cut the potatoes in half and arrange on 4 chilled plates. Top with the fava beans and diced smoked salmon. Sprinkle with sea salt flakes, cracked black pepper, and chives. Drizzle with about 1 tablespoon of extra virgin olive oil per plate and sprinkle with 1 teaspoon vinegar, then serve.

Salade niçoise

10 red new potatoes

8 quail eggs or small hen eggs

1 cup shelled fava beans, fresh or frozen,
or 6 cooked baby artichokes, halved

4 oz. green beans, topped and tailed

3 scallions, halved lengthwise

2 small red onions, halved lengthwise

1 kirby cucumber, unwaxed

2 red or yellow bell peppers,
peeled (see method)

6–8 inner leaves from 1 romaine lettuce

1 pint cherry tomatoes, about 20, halved

8–12 canned anchovy fillets
or 4 oz. tuna, drained

about 20 Niçoise black olives, pitted

about 20 caperberries or 3 tablespoons
salt-packed capers, rinsed and drained

a large handful of fresh basil leaves

olive oil, for tossing

VINAIGRETTE

6 tablespoons extra virgin olive oil

1 tablespoon white wine vinegar,
cider vinegar or sherry vinegar

1 teaspoon Dijon mustard (optional)

1 garlic clove, crushed

kosher salt or sea salt and freshly
ground black pepper

SERVES 4 AS AN APPETIZER,
8 AS AN ENTRÉE

Cook the new potatoes in boiling salted water until tender, about 10 minutes. Drain and plunge them into a bowl of ice water with ice cubes. Let cool. Drain, then toss in a little olive oil and cut in half.

Boil the quail eggs for 1½ minutes, then drain and plunge into cold water. Peel in a bowl of cold water. (They can be difficult to peel: you need to crack the shell and also pierce the very tough skin underneath. The water will help separate the skin.) Cut in half just before serving.

Microwave the fava beans on full for 3 minutes if fresh or 2 minutes if frozen. Plunge into ice water, then pop each bean out of its gray skin. Microwave the green beans for 2 minutes, then plunge into ice water. Alternatively, steam the both kinds of beans until tender.

Blanch the scallions for 30 seconds in boiling water. Drain and plunge into ice water.

Finely slice the onions and cucumber, preferably on a mandoline— slice the cucumber diagonally. If peeling the bell peppers, do so using a vegetable peeler, then cut into thick strips.

Put the lettuce leaves on a platter. Make bundles of blanched green beans and tie up with blanched scallion leaves. Add the potatoes, eggs, tomatoes, cucumber, onions, and bell pepper. Top with anchovy fillets or tuna, black olives, caperberries or capers, and basil leaves. Mix the vinaigrette ingredients in a small pitcher and serve separately.

A wonderful lunch for four or an appetizer for eight. Choose small, delicious, interesting potatoes—or leave them out. Quail eggs are pretty and fun to use instead of hen eggs. Use your choice of the other ingredients: the basics are the anchovies or tuna, plus the beans, lettuce, tomatoes, olives, and onions.

Thai spicy shrimp salad

This salad is very simple—you can also make it with pre-cooked shrimp. When preparing the lemongrass and kaffir lime leaves, make sure to slice them very finely indeed. If you can't find them, use a squeeze of lemon juice and some grated lime zest instead.

1 tablespoon peanut oil

12 raw medium shrimp, shelled, deveined and halved lengthwise

1 stalk lemongrass, very finely chopped

a handful of fresh cilantro leaves, finely chopped

2 pink Thai shallots or 1 small regular shallot, finely sliced lengthwise

3 scallions, finely chopped

1 red chile, finely sliced and seeded if preferred

2 kaffir lime leaves, mid-rib removed, the leaves very finely sliced crosswise, then finely chopped

12 cherry tomatoes, halved

a handful of mint sprigs, to serve

THAI DRESSING

4 tablespoons fish sauce

juice of 1 lemon or 2 limes

2 teaspoons brown sugar

2 tablespoons red Thai curry paste

SERVES 4

Heat the oil in a wok or large, heavy skillet, add the shrimp, and stir-fry for about 1 minute until opaque. Let cool.

Put the dressing ingredients in a bowl and beat well with a fork until the sugar dissolves. Add the shrimp and all the other ingredients except the mint sprigs. Toss, then serve, topped with mint.

Vietnamese chicken salad

4 handfuls of bean sprouts, rinsed and drained

1 small carrot

6 scallions, halved, then finely sliced lengthwise

a handful of fresh mint leaves, preferably Vietnamese mint

a handful of Asian basil leaves (optional)

2 tablespoons roasted peanuts, finely chopped

POACHED CHICKEN

2 chicken breasts, on the bone

1 inch fresh ginger, sliced

1 garlic clove, crushed

1 tablespoon fish sauce or a pinch of salt

1 red chile, sliced

2 scallions, sliced

boiling chicken stock or water, to cover

CHILE-LIME DRESSING

⅓ cup freshly squeezed lime juice, about 2–3 limes

1 tablespoon fish sauce

2 tablespoons brown sugar

1 green chile, halved, seeded, and finely chopped

1 red chile, halved, seeded, and finely chopped

1 garlic clove, crushed

1 inch fresh ginger, peeled and grated

SERVES 4

You can use any cooked chicken for this salad. However, poaching is a very healthy way of cooking: there is no added fat, and much of what's there melts away as the chicken cooks. This salad isn't authentic — that would involve stir-fried chicken mince — but it's easy and it tastes fresh and good, like most Vietnamese food. If you can't find Vietnamese mint and Asian basil, you can substitute ordinary mint, but not ordinary basil (just leave it out).

Put the chicken in a wide saucepan, add the ginger, garlic, fish sauce or salt, chile, and scallions. Add chicken stock or water to cover and return to a boil. Reduce the heat, cover with a lid, and simmer, without boiling, until the chicken is tender, about 15–20 minutes. Remove from the heat and let cool in the liquid. Remove from the liquid, take the meat off the bone, discard bone and skin, then pull the chicken into long shreds. Reserve the cooking liquid for another use, such as soup.

Mix all the dressing ingredients in a screw-top bottle and shake to mix.

To trim the bean sprouts, pinch off the tails and remove the bean from between the two leaves (optional.)

To prepare the carrot, peel and shred into long matchsticks on a mandoline or the large blade of a box grater.

Pile the bean sprouts on 4 plates. Add the carrot and chicken and top with the scallions, mint, and basil leaves, if using. Sprinkle with the dressing and roasted peanuts, then serve.

Insalata gonzaga

A marvelous, simple chicken salad named after the Gonzagas, who were the Dukes of Mantua, near Modena, the home of balsamic vinegar. True balsamic vinegar is rare and expensive, but use the best you can afford. This recipe comes from my young Italian cousin who can turn out utterly delicious dishes seemingly without effort.

1 cup pine nuts

⅓ cup extra virgin olive oil, preferably from Tuscany or Umbria

1 tablespoon wine vinegar, red or white

1 lb. skinless, boneless, roasted chicken breasts

2 small red radicchio lettuces, leaves separated

¼ cup raisins

1–2 tablespoons balsamic vinegar

kosher salt or sea salt and freshly cracked black pepper

4 oz. fresh Parmesan cheese, at room temperature, cut into shards, to serve

SERVES 4

Put the pine nuts in a dry skillet and heat, stirring, until lightly golden. Remove to a plate.

Put the oil and vinegar in a salad bowl, add a pinch of salt, and beat with a fork. Slice the chicken or pull it into shreds. Add the chicken and radicchio to the bowl and toss gently.

Serve on salad plates, sprinkle with the raisins, pepper and balsamic vinegar and top with shards of Parmesan.

Note: For this salad, I soaked the raisins in verjuice for 10 minutes before adding to the salad. Verjuice is halfway between vinegar and wine—delicious, if a little difficult to find. Omit if necessary, or use wine.

Rare beef salad
with parsley oil and wasabi mayonnaise

A splendid special-occasion salad for a summer lunch party. When you serve it, cut slices of beef about ½ inch thick: there's nothing worse than mean little paper-thin slices—it always looks as though you bought them at a deli. For the best flavor, let the meat return to room temperature before serving (it only takes a few minutes.) Increase the amount of fillet to cater for the number of guests—since it's the same thickness, it will take the same amount of time in the oven, no matter how big it is.

1 beef fillet, about 20 inches long, well trimmed

8 oz. peppery leaves, such as watercress or wild arugula

kosher salt or sea salt and freshly ground black pepper

olive oil, for searing

PARSLEY OIL
a bunch of parsley
1 cup extra virgin olive oil

WASABI MAYONNAISE
1 cup homemade mayonnaise (page 62)
2–3 tablespoons wasabi paste (about 1 tube)

SERVES 12

To make the parsley oil, put the parsley and olive oil in a blender and blend until smooth. Set aside for 30 minutes or overnight in the refrigerator.

Preheat the oven to 400°F. Brush a heavy-based roasting pan with olive oil and heat on top of the stove until very hot. Add the beef and sear on all sides until nicely browned. Transfer to the oven and roast for 20 minutes. Remove from the oven and set aside to fix the juices. Sprinkle with salt and pepper.

Let the meat cool to room temperature and reserve any cooking juices. If preparing in advance, wrap closely in foil and chill, but return it and the parsley oil to room temperature before serving.

Arrange the leaves down the middle of a rectangular or oval serving dish. Slice the beef into ½-inch thick slices with a very sharp carving knife (or an electric knife). Arrange in overlapping slices on top of the leaves and pour any cooking juices from the pan or carving board over the top.

Drizzle the parsley oil, strained if necessary, over the beef. Mix the mayonnaise with the wasabi paste and serve separately.

BEANS GRAINS AND NOODLES

Quick couscous salad

This very quick and easy salad is endlessly adaptable, and great if you want to take your lunch to work. I prefer wholegrain couscous, but use regular if you like. Easy-cook couscous is supposed to be just soaked then drained, but I find it's better for a little more steaming or microwaving after soaking.

¼ cup easy-cook wholegrain couscous

½ cup boiling chicken stock or water

1 cooked chicken breast, pulled into shreds

3 halves sun-dried tomatoes in oil, drained or 6 fresh cherry tomatoes, halved

2 marinated artichoke hearts, sliced

3–4 scallions, sliced

2 cups canned chickpeas, (15 oz.), rinsed and drained

2–3 tablespoons extra virgin olive oil or 1 tablespoon pumpkin oil

1 teaspoon white rice vinegar or wine vinegar

1 teaspoon Dijon mustard (optional)

kosher salt or sea salt and freshly ground black pepper

a handful of flat-leaf parsley, coarsely chopped, or a few sprigs of watercress

SERVES 2

Put the couscous in a non-metal bowl and cover with the stock or water. Leave for 15 minutes until the water has been absorbed. For a fluffier texture, put the soaked couscous in a strainer and steam over simmering water for another 10 minutes, or microwave in the bowl on 50 percent for about 5 minutes. Drain if necessary, pressing the liquid through the strainer with a spoon. Let cool.

When ready to make up the salad, put a layer of couscous in a lidded plastic container, then add a layer of chicken. Add the tomatoes, artichoke hearts, scallions, and chickpeas. Keep the leaves in a separate container until just before serving.

Put the oil in a screw-top bottle, add the vinegar, mustard, if using, salt, and pepper and mix well. Sprinkle over the salad. Cover and carry.

To serve, add the parsley and watercress and toss well.

Tonno e fagioli
Italian tuna and beans

1 large tuna steak, about 8 oz.,
or 2 small cans good-quality tuna,
about 6 oz. each, drained

⅓ cup olive oil, plus extra for brushing

2 red onions, finely sliced

2–3 fat garlic cloves, crushed

1 tablespoon sherry vinegar or
white wine vinegar

4 cups cooked or canned green flageolet
beans, white cannellini beans, or a mixture

4 handfuls of fresh basil leaves
and small sprigs

kosher salt or sea salt and freshly
ground black pepper

SERVES 6 AS AN APPETIZER,
4 AS AN ENTRÉE

I first tasted this dish in a restaurant on the edge of the piazza in Siena with my 10-year-old Italian cousin. White cannellini beans are usual, but I like the taste and pretty color of green flageolets. Fresh tuna can be expensive, so this recipe is a good way of making one wonderful tuna steak stretch a little further.

If using fresh tuna, brush with olive oil and put on a preheated stove-top grill pan. Cook for 3 minutes on each side or until barred with brown but pink in the middle (the time depends on the thickness of the fish.) Remove from the pan, cool, and pull into chunks.

Put the oil, onions, crushed garlic, and vinegar in a bowl and beat with a fork. Add the beans and toss until well coated.

Add the tuna and basil, salt, and pepper, then serve with crusty bread and Italian red wine.

Vietnamese table salad
with herbs, vegetables, and noodles

A do-it-yourself salad platter is served with every Vietnamese meal. Some people think the idea was borrowed from the French, but in fact it is indigenous. The combinations of vegetables are almost infinite and the herbs give a fresh, scented flavor. To eat, take a lettuce leaf from the platter, add your choice of herbs and other ingredients, then wrap the leaf into a package and dip in the spicy sauce.

2 teaspoons white rice vinegar

2 teaspoons sugar

½ teaspoon kosher salt or sea salt

2 large carrots, cut into matchstick strips

about 8 inches cucumber, halved lengthwise

2 oz. beanthread noodles (optional)

small inner leaves from a romaine lettuce or 1 iceberg lettuce, leaves separated

6 scallions, shredded

a handful of bean sprouts, rinsed and trimmed

a bunch of cilantro

a bunch of mint, leaves only

a bunch of Asian basil—not sweet basil— leaves only (optional)

NUÓC CHAM DIPPING SAUCE

2 garlic cloves, crushed

1 red chile, seeded and chopped

1 tablespoon brown sugar

juice of ½ lime

¼ cup fish sauce

1 small red or green chile, sliced, to serve

SERVES 4

Put the vinegar, sugar, and salt in a bowl, add 1 cup water and the strips of carrot, stir well, and set aside for 30 minutes or up to 24 hours. Drain.

Finely slice the cucumber halves diagonally into half-moons.

If using noodles, bring a large saucepan of water to a boil, add the noodles, and stir to separate. Boil for 2 minutes, then drain and transfer to a bowl of ice water until ready to use.

To make the *Nuóc Cham*, mash the garlic, chile, and sugar with a mortar and pestle to form a paste. Stir in the lime juice, fish sauce, and ¼ cup water. Taste and add extra water if preferred and put into a small dipping bowl. Add the sliced chile.

Arrange the lettuce leaves in the middle of a large serving platter, then put piles of drained carrot, cucumber, scallions, bean sprouts, and herbs around the outside. Drain the noodles, if using, and put in a separate bowl.

To eat, take a lettuce leaf, add your choice of other ingredients, then roll up. Dip in the *Nuóc Cham* and eat.

Soba noodles, made from buckwheat, are wonderful cold, served on flat baskets or in slatted wooden boxes. Other Japanese noodles, such as white somen noodles or the larger, ribbon-like udon, are also delicious served this way. I particularly like the beautiful green-tea-flavored, pale green, cha-soba noodles ("cha" means "tea" in many languages.)

Japanese soba noodle salad

14 oz. dried soba noodles

12 dried shiitake mushrooms

2 tablespoons Japanese soy sauce

2 tablespoons mirin
(Japanese sweet rice wine) or sherry

12 uncooked shrimp

12 scallions, finely sliced

4 teaspoons furokaki pepper (optional)

4 teaspoons wasabi paste, to serve

DIPPING SAUCE

1 cup dashi stock*

2 tablespoons mirin

a pinch of sugar

3 tablespoons Japanese soy sauce

SERVES 4

*Dashi stock is available in powder or concentrate form in Asian stores. Dissolve 1 teaspoon in 1 cup hot (not boiling) water, or to taste.

Put the dipping sauce ingredients in a saucepan, simmer for about 5 minutes, then chill.

Cook the noodles for 5–6 minutes or according to the package instructions. Drain, rinse in cold water, and cool over ice. Chill.

Put the shiitakes in a saucepan, cover with 1 cup boiling water, and soak until soft. Remove and discard the mushroom stems. Add the soy sauce and mirin to the pan, bring to a boil and simmer for a few minutes to meld the flavors. Add the shrimp and simmer for about 1 minute until firm. Drain, reserving the cooking liquid. Shell the shrimp, but leave the tail fins intact. Devein and cut each shrimp down the back to the fin, giving a butterfly shape. Chill the shrimp and poaching liquid. Just before serving, dunk the chilled noodles in the liquid, then drain.

To serve, put a layer of ice cubes in a slatted wood box or bowl, then add the noodles. Add the shrimp, scallions, and mushrooms. Sprinkle with furokaki pepper, if using. Serve with separate dishes of wasabi paste and dipping sauce.

Chickpea lunchbox salad

Chickpeas (garbanzo beans) are the basis of my favorite lunchbox salads. You can prepare them in advance, so the dressing soaks into the chickpeas, then add the fresh ingredients just before serving. You can add any number of other ingredients, including olives, prosciutto, salami or chorizo, canned tuna, other vegetables, leaves or herbs, and perhaps spices. Whatever takes your fancy in your Italian gourmet store.

2 cups cooked or canned chickpeas, rinsed and drained

4 oz. marinated artichoke hearts

4 oz. sun-dried tomatoes in oil, drained (optional)

about 20 very ripe cherry tomatoes, halved

6 scallions, finely sliced diagonally

leaves from 4 sprigs of basil, torn

a small bunch of chives, snipped with shears

leaves from 4 sprigs of flat-leaf parsley, chopped

1 cup, about 2 oz., fresh Parmesan, shaved

1 tablespoon black pepper, cracked with a mortar and pestle

DRESSING

⅓ cup extra virgin olive oil

1 tablespoon freshly squeezed lemon juice or sherry vinegar

1 teaspoon Dijon mustard (optional)

1 small garlic clove, crushed

kosher salt or sea salt and freshly ground black pepper

SERVES 4

Put the dressing ingredients in a screw-top jar and shake well.

Put the chickpeas, artichoke hearts, and drained, sun-dried tomatoes, if using, in a bowl or lunchbox. Pour over the dressing. Cover with a lid and chill for up to 4 hours.

When ready to serve, add the cherry tomatoes, scallions, basil, chives, and parsley. Stir gently, then sprinkle with the shaved Parmesan and pepper.

Note: Sun-blushed tomatoes (partially-dried sun-dried tomatoes) are sold in Italian gourmet stores. If you can find them, try them in this recipe.

FRUITS

Watermelon and feta salad
with ginger and chillies

I adore watermelons—they were a school picnic treat where I grew up and they have never lost their romance in my eyes. I love them by themselves, in crushes and smoothies—and also as a savory salad with salty cheese and cracked pepper.

4 thick slices watermelon

8 oz. feta cheese or
4 oz. Parmesan

1 tablespoon black peppercorns

1 inch fresh ginger, peeled

juice of 1 lime

2 tablespoons nut oil
or extra virgin olive oil

1 red chile, seeded
and finely sliced

kosher salt or sea salt flakes

SERVES 4

Cut the watermelon slices into triangular wedges and remove the seeds. Cut the feta cheese into long shards or crumble into large pieces. If using Parmesan, shave it into long pieces with a vegetable peeler. Coarsely crush the peppercorns. Grate the ginger and squeeze the juice from the gratings into a small pitcher (you can also press it through a garlic crusher.) Add the lime juice and oil and beat with a fork.

Arrange the watermelon pieces on a plate or in a bowl, standing them vertically. Add the feta or Parmesan, crushed peppercorns, and a little salt. Sprinkle with the ginger dressing and sliced chile, then serve.

Asian pear salad
with macadamias and macadamia nut oil

Toast the sesame seeds in a dry skillet for about 1 minute, stirring, until lightly golden. Set aside.

Blanch the beans in boiling salted water for about 3 minutes or until *al dente*. Remove and plunge into ice water. Let cool, then drain and pat dry. Put the olive oil in a bowl, then add the beans, chiles, and leaves. Toss gently to coat.

Slice the pears into wedges, cut off the cores, then brush the wedges with the lime juice. Add to the bowl and toss gently to coat.

Arrange piles of the dressed salad on 4 small plates. Sprinkle with the nuts, sesame seeds, salt, and black pepper. Drizzle with macadamia oil and serve.

1 tablespoon white sesame seeds

4 oz. snake beans (Chinese long beans), cut into 2-inch lengths, or French beans

1 tablespoon extra virgin olive oil

2 red chiles, finely sliced

about 1 cup arugula

about 4 cups other salad leaves

2 Asian pears or 4 red-skinned pears

juice of 1 lime

1 cup macadamia nuts, preferably unsalted

¼ cup macadamia nut oil or olive oil

kosher salt or sea salt and freshly ground black pepper

SERVES 4

Macadamia nuts are native to Queensland, Australia and, since I am too, this salad is in honor of my home state. You can use your favorite nuts: but try to match nut and oil, hazelnuts and hazelnut oil, or walnuts and walnut oil—or just use more extra virgin olive oil if you can't find the appropriate nut oil. Keep nut oils in the refrigerator, because they are very delicate and can go rancid very quickly (as can the nuts themselves, so store them there too.)

Papaya salsa

Serve this fresh and juicy salad with kabobs of char-grilled tuna, poached chicken, or grilled meats. It's also terrific with tortilla or pita wraps. I like papaya, but you could use other fruits instead—like avocado, apple, or Asian pear (brushed with lemon juice to stop them browning)—or perhaps pineapple or watermelon.

1 medium papaya, about 8 oz.

1 red and 1 yellow bell pepper

1 inch fresh ginger, peeled and grated

1 red chile, seeded and diced

6 baby cornichons (gherkins), finely sliced

½ cup torn fresh cilantro leaves

grated zest and juice of 3 limes

kosher salt or sea salt and freshly ground black pepper

SERVES 4–6

Peel the papaya with a vegetable peeler, cut it in half lengthwise and scoop out the seeds, then dice the flesh and put in a bowl.

Peel the bell peppers with a vegetable peeler, seed, and dice. Add to the bowl, then add the ginger, diced chile, and cornichons. Stir in the cilantro, lime zest, and juice, and set aside for about 10 minutes to develop the flavors.

Serve with meat, fish, or poultry.

Moroccan orange salad
with mint, harissa, and red onion

Variations of this Moroccan classic can be made with orange flower water in the dressing, or with crushed cardamom instead of cinnamon, or nutmeg and cloves. Make sure you cut off all the white pith from the orange before slicing—the pith is very bitter and spoils the salad.

3 oranges

1 red onion, halved lengthwise, then finely sliced into narrow wedges

a handful of mint sprigs

1 teaspoon ground cinnamon or mild chile powder

ORANGE DRESSING

juice from the oranges (see method)

2 tablespoons fruity extra virgin olive oil

1 teaspoon harissa paste*

kosher salt or sea salt and freshly ground black pepper

SERVES 4

*North African hot pepper paste available from ethnic grocers and specialty markets

Grate the zest of 1 of the oranges and put in a bowl. Cut a thick slice off the top and bottom of each orange. Squeeze the juice out of the tops and bottoms and add to the bowl. Set the fruit flat on a cutting board. With a very sharp knife, cut off the orange peel in sections from top to bottom, making sure you remove all the white pith. Slice the oranges thinly crosswise saving any juice and pouring it into the bowl. Squeeze the juice from 1-2 slices and add it to the bowl.

Arrange the orange slices on a flat plate, top with the onion and mint sprigs, and sprinkle with cinnamon or chile powder.

Add the olive oil, harissa paste, salt, and pepper to the bowl of orange juice, mix well, sprinkle over the salad, then serve.

1 large ripe papaya, about 16 inches long, or several smaller ones

1 ripe pineapple

6 ripe passionfruit with wrinkled skin (optional)

2 ripe bananas

other exotic tropical fruits, as available, such as Asian pears, roseapples, kiwi, cactus fruit, pink guavas, lychees, longans, or pomelo segments, all prepared as required

sour cream or ice cream, to serve

THAI GINGER DRESSING

1¼ cups sugar, brown or granulated

grated zest and juice of 3 limes or 1 lemon

1–2 inches fresh ginger, peeled and grated

SERVES 4 OR MORE

To make the dressing, put all the ingredients in a saucepan, add 1 cup water, bring to a boil, and simmer until the sugar has dissolved and the liquid is a light syrup. Remove from the heat and let cool.

Peel the papaya with a vegetable peeler, cut in half lengthwise and remove and discard the seeds. Cut the flesh into large cubes. Put in a bowl with any juice.

Cut the top and bottom off the pineapple, stand it on its base, then slice off the skin. Remove all the prickly eyes. Cut the pineapple into 4 wedges, then slice off the cores. Cut 1 of the wedges into bite-size triangles. Add to the bowl with any juice. Crush the remaining pineapple in a blender or juicer and add to the bowl.

Open the passionfruit, if using, and scrape the seeds into the salad.

Add your choice of the other fruit, but reserve the bananas until later. Sprinkle with the dressing and chill for at least 1 hour. When ready to serve, slice in the banana and serve with sour cream or ice cream.

Tropical fruit salad
with Thai ginger dressing

I grew up in sub-tropical Australia, so I think that fruit salad should always be based on tropical fruits, especially pineapple and papaya. Choose whatever is available where you live, but include at least some tropicals. Some fruits, such as bananas, go "furry" in juice, so should be added at the last minute. If you prefer a clearer sauce, make the dressing with white sugar rather than brown.

DRESSINGS

Pesto

½ cup extra virgin olive oil

¼ cup pine nuts

6 garlic cloves, crushed

1 teaspoon kosher salt or sea salt

a large bunch of fresh basil leaves, torn

½ cup freshly grated Parmesan cheese, about 2 oz.

½ cup freshly grated pecorino cheese, about 2 oz.

MAKES ABOUT 1 CUP

Brush a skillet with a little of the olive oil, add the pine nuts, and sauté gently and quickly until golden (about 30 seconds). They burn very easily, so don't leave them. Let cool. Transfer to a food processor, add the garlic, salt, and basil and blend to a paste. Add the Parmesan, blend again, then add the oil and pecorino and blend again until smooth.

CILANTRO PESTO

For a Middle Eastern flavor, omit the basil and use half parsley and half cilantro. Omit the pine nuts and use almonds instead.

ARUGULA PESTO

Use half parsley and half arugula leaves instead of the basil. Use all Parmesan instead of a mixture of cheeses.

PARSLEY PESTO

A much milder version using parsley instead of basil leaves.

RED PESTO

Instead of basil, use 8 oz. sun-dried tomatoes bottled in olive oil, drained. A teaspoon of harissa paste will lift the flavor even further. (Buy spicy harissa paste from ethnic stores.)

Asian dressings

Asian dressings are particularly delicious—and healthful because they often contain no oil. These include the Peanut Sauce (page 20), Chile-Lime Dressing (page 34), Thai Dressing (page 32) and *Nuóc Cham* Dipping Sauce (page 45), which is also good as a dressing.

SESAME OIL DRESSING

1 inch fresh ginger, peeled and sliced

3 scallions, chopped and quartered crosswise

1 red chile, seeded and chopped

¾ cup peanut oil

¼ cup sesame oil

1 tablespoon Szechuan peppercorns

Put the ginger, scallions, chile and peppercorns in a small blender and pulse to chop. Put the peanut and sesame oils in a saucepan and heat until hot but not smoking. Remove from the heat, add the flavorings, stir, cover with a lid, let cool, then strain. Serve tossed through blanched vegetables and with chicken or noodle salads. The dressing may also be marinated overnight before straining.

LIME DRESSING

1 tablespoon fish sauce

juice of 1 lime

1 teaspoon brown sugar

Mix in a small bowls and serve as a dipping sauce, or sprinkled over the salad.

Mayonnaise

The key to making mayonnaise is to have all the ingredients at room temperature, and to add the oil a few drops at a time at first, then more quickly, but not in a continuous stream as many books advise. The emulsion needs time to absorb the oil, so don't overtax it. Don't use all olive oil (unless you're making aioli)—the flavor is too strong. Use a light oil such as sunflower, but good quality: don't use those labeled just "vegetable oil." I use a food processor to make mayonnaise but, if you're a purist, by all means make it by hand.

2 egg yolks, at room temperature
1 whole egg (if making in a food processor)
2 teaspoons Dijon mustard
a large pinch of salt
2 teaspoons freshly squeezed lemon juice or white wine vinegar
1 cup good-quality sunflower, peanut, or safflower oil
½ cup virgin olive oil
MAKES ABOUT 2 CUPS

Put the eggs, mustard, salt, and lemon juice in a food processor and blend until pale. Gradually add the oil, a few drops at a time at first, then more quickly, but in stages, leaving a few seconds between additions to allow the eggs to "digest" the oil. When all the oil has been added, if the mixture is too thick, add about 1 tablespoon warm water. Serve immediately, or press a sheet of plastic wrap over the surface to prevent a skin from forming. It may be refrigerated for up to 3 days.

AIOLI

An unctuous garlic mayonnaise served with Provençal dishes such as Salade Niçoise.

Crush 4 garlic cloves into a food processor at the same time as the eggs. Proceed as in the main recipe (use all olive oil if preferred).

Also delicious with 1 tablespoon harissa paste added (a quick version of rouille.)

GREEN GODDESS DRESSING

Put 1 cup mayonnaise in a food processor. Add 2 oz. canned anchovies, salt, pepper, 2 tablespoons each of tarragon, parsley, and chives, 1 tablespoon fresh lemon juice, and 3 tablespoons vinegar. Process until smooth.

Vinaigrette

5 tablespoons extra virgin olive oil

1 tablespoon white wine vinegar

1 teaspoon Dijon mustard (optional)

kosher salt or sea salt and freshly ground black pepper

MAKES ABOUT ½ CUP

Put all the ingredients in a salad bowl and beat with a fork or small whisk. Alternatively, put in a screw-top jar and shake to form an emulsion.

VARIATIONS

I like to use Japanese rice vinegar, which gives a mild, smooth taste. You can also substitute red wine vinegar, sherry vinegar, cider vinegar, or others. Freshly squeezed lime or lemon juice are also traditional replacements for the vinegar.

A crushed garlic clove is often added to the vinaigrette. Delicious, but death to the breath.

Some people like to include a little sugar in the dressing. I think this is only necessary if you've used too much vinegar.

Instead of extra virgin, use 2 tablespoons mild virgin olive oil and 3 tablespoons nut oil such as walnut, macadamia, or hazelnut. Nut oils turn rancid very quickly, so buy small quantities, always keep them in the fridge and use quickly (keep the nuts there too).

A warm vinaigrette poured over salad leaves, meat, fish, or vegetables is also delicious.

One of the nicest dressings of all is just a sprinkle of the very best quality extra virgin olive oil.

index

conversion charts

Weights and measures have been rounded up
or down slightly to make measuring easier.

VOLUME EQUIVALENTS:

American	Metric	Imperial
1 teaspoon	5 ml	
1 tablespoon	15 ml	
¼ cup	60 ml	2 fl.oz.
⅓ cup	75 ml	2½ fl.oz.
½ cup	125 ml	4 fl.oz.
⅔ cup	150 ml	5 fl.oz. (¼ pint)
¾ cup	175 ml	6 fl.oz.
1 cup	250 ml	8 fl.oz.

WEIGHT EQUIVALENTS:

Imperial	Metric
1 oz.	25 g
2 oz.	50 g
3 oz.	75 g
4 oz.	125 g
5 oz.	150 g
6 oz.	175 g
7 oz.	200 g
8 oz. (½ lb.)	250 g
9 oz.	275 g
10 oz.	300 g
11 oz.	325 g
12 oz.	375 g
13 oz.	400 g
14 oz.	425 g
15 oz.	475 g
16 oz. (1 lb.)	500 g
2 lb.	1 kg

MEASUREMENTS:

Inches	Cm
¼ inch	5 mm
½ inch	1 cm
¾ inch	1.5 cm
1 inch	2.5 cm
2 inches	5 cm
3 inches	7 cm
4 inches	10 cm
5 inches	12 cm
6 inches	15 cm
7 inches	18 cm
8 inches	20 cm
9 inches	23 cm
10 inches	25 cm
11 inches	28 cm
12 inches	30 cm

OVEN TEMPERATURES:

110°C	(225°F)	Gas ¼
120°C	(250°F)	Gas ½
140°C	(275°F)	Gas 1
150°C	(300°F)	Gas 2
160°C	(325°F)	Gas 3
180°C	(350°F)	Gas 4
190°C	(375°F)	Gas 5
200°C	(400°F)	Gas 6
220°C	(425°F)	Gas 7
230°C	(450°F)	Gas 8
240°C	(475°F)	Gas 9